Rainald Bierstedt
Learn English: read and enjoy classic short stories by
British writers. Band 1
*Anbei: Vokabelhilfen, Übungsaufgaben,
Background Informationen.*

AF211199

Rainald Bierstedt

Learn English:

read and enjoy

classic short stories

by British writers.

Anbei:
Vokabelhilfen, Übungsaufgaben,
Background Informationen

Bibliografische Information der Deutschen Nationalbibliothek:
Die Deutsche Nationalbibliothek verzeichnet diese Publikation in der
Deutschen Nationalbibliografie; detaillierte bibliografische Daten sind
im Internet über http://dnb.d-nb.de abrufbar.

Verlag:
BoD · Books on Demand GmbH, Überseering 33, 22297 Hamburg,
bod@bod.de

Druck:
Libri Plureos GmbH, Friedensallee 273, 22763 Hamburg

ISBN: 978-3-7693-7661-6

In dieser Publikation werden nur lizenzfreie Bilder verwendet.

Contents - Inhalt

Einleitung: Lesetipps

Oft wird die Frage gestellt, ob man durch das Lesen von Büchern wirklich Englisch lernen kann. Aus Erfahrungen kann ich bestätigen, dass insbesondere Short Stories gut geeignet sind für das Lernen und Vervollkommnen der englischen Sprache. So kann man den Wortschatz erweitern, indem man Vokabeln und Redewendungen im Zusammenhang mit einer Story liest. Zudem lernt man Grammatik in der Praxis kennen und entwickelt ein besseres Sprachgefühl für Satzbau und Wortwahl. Ebenso wichtig ist, dass man beim Lesen tiefer in die englische Kultur eindringen kann.

Das vorliegende Buch enthält 5 Short Stories bekannter britischer Autoren. Einige Texte sind im Sinne des Lernens leicht gekürzt. Der Inhalt wird jedoch dadurch nicht beeinträchtigt.

Vokabeltipps sind als Hilfen eingearbeitet. Background-Informationen sowie Übungsaufgaben, inklusive Lösungsvorschläge, sind ebenfalls dabei.

Bevor man mit dem Lesen beginnt, ist es ratsam, sich über folgende Lesestrategien Gedanken zu machen:

1. Orientierendes Lesen.

Man überfliegt den Text, um einen ersten Eindruck vom Inhalt zu bekommen. Dabei muss man nicht unbedingt jedes Wort nachschlagen/übersetzen. Vieles lässt sich aus dem Kontext erschließen. Vordergründig ist es, sich einen Überblick zu verschaffen, um herauszufinden, worum es eigentlich in der Story geht.

2. Vertiefendes Lesen.

Man sollte den Text ruhig mehrere Male lesen, um möglichst den ganzen Inhalt sowie auch Einzelheiten zu verstehen.

3. Suchendes Lesen.

Jetzt kommt es darauf an, nach bestimmten Informationen/Schlüsselwörtern im Text suchen. Dazu erfolgen pro Short Story einige Anregungen, wie z.B. Fragestellungen zum Textinhalt oder kleine Quizrunden.

In diesem Sinne, genießt diese literarischen Werke, habt Freude daran.

Start

reading

Short Story 1:

"The Adventure of Charles A. Milverton"

by Sir Arthur Conan Doyle

Holmes and I *(Watson)* returned about six o'clock on a cold, frosty winter's evening. As Holmes turned up the lamp the light fell upon a card on the table. He threw it on the floor.

I picked it up and read: CHARLES AUGUSTUS MILVERTON, Appledore Towers, Hampstead. "Who is he?" I asked. "The worst man in London," Holmes answered. "Is anything on the back of the card?" I turned it over.

"Will come at 6:30 -- C.A.M.," I read. "But why?" "I'll tell you, Watson. He is the king of all the blackmailers." **(1. see words below)** I had seldom heard my friend speak with such intensity of feeling. "And why will he come here?"

"Because a famous client has placed her case in my hands. It is the Lady Eva Blackwell, the most beautiful debutante of last theatre season. She will be married in a fortnight (2) to the Earl of Dovercourt. Milverton has several letters from her in his hand. Eva wrote some love letters to a young man years ago. Milverton wants to get a large sum of money or he will send the letters to the Earl."

Words:
(1) Erpresser.
(2) in 14 Tagen.

A minute later Milverton was in the room. He said, "You say that you are acting for Lady Eva. Will she accept my <u>terms</u>?" (3) "What are your terms?" "Seven thousand pounds."

"It is impossible," said Holmes. Holmes thought for a little. Then he continued, "Lady Eva is not a wealthy woman. Please moderate your demands, and that you will return the letters at this price, the highest that you can get." Milverton got up, took up his coat, laid his hand on his revolver, and turned to the door. Milverton left the room, Holmes sat <u>motionless</u> (4) by the fire.

For half an hour he was <u>silent and still</u>. (5) Then, with the gesture of a man who has taken his decision, he sprang to his feet and passed into his bedroom. A little later, he came back dressed as a young workman. "I'll be back some time, Watson," said he, and <u>vanished</u> (6) into the night. For some days Holmes came and went at all hours in this dress. At last, however, on a wild, stormy evening.

Words:
(3) Bedingungen.
(4) regungslos.
(5) schweigend und still.
(6) verschwand.

He returned from his last expedition. "You'll be interested to hear that I'm <u>engaged</u>." (7) "My dear friend! I congratu…" He, "Engaged to Milverton's housemaid." "Good heavens, Holmes!" He, "I am a <u>plumber</u> (8), Escott, by name. I have walked out with her each evening, and I have talked about her house as I know like my own." "But the girl, Holmes?" "Watson, I plan to break in Milverton's house tonight, to look for the letters." "For heaven's sake, Holmes, think what you are doing," I cried. "Holmes, you will be in such a difficult position."

"Well, that is part of the risk. Watson, it's also a sporting duel between Milverton and me." "Well, I don't like it, but it must be," said I. "When do we start?" "We shall start before midnight. Milverton is a heavy sleeper."

Holmes and I put on our dress-clothes and left the house in Baker Street. These documents are contained in a safe in his study room. Agatha, Holmes's "bride", said it is almost impossible to wake the master. Some minutes later we were in Milverton's study.

Words:
(7) verlobt.
(8) Klempner.

Holmes looked for a safe with the letters, found it. Finally, I heard a click, and the green safe door swung open, and inside I saw many paper packets. Suddenly he stopped, listened carefully, and shut the safe door again and collected his instruments.

Holmes and I had to hide behind the window curtain. There was a noise somewhere in the house. The door opened. What a surprise. Right in front of us, we saw the rounded back of Milverton. Several times I had observed that Milverton looked at his watch. Suddenly, everyone knocked on the door. Milverton opened it. "Well," said he, "you are nearly half an hour late." In front of him, there stood a tall, slim, dark woman, a <u>veil</u> (9) over her face, she wore a long coat. "Oh, great heavens, who are you?"

The woman, without a word, <u>had raised</u> (10) her veil from her chin. "Yes, it's me! The Countess Albert," she said, "the woman whose life you have ruined."
Milverton laughed. "And so, you sent the letters to my husband, you broke him his heart and he died." "You will ruin no more lives as you have ruined mine. Take that, you hound -- and that! -- and that! -- and that!"

Words:
(9) Schleier.
(10) hatte angehoben/gelüftet.

She had drawn a little revolver and shot 4 times into Milverton's body. I heard opening the door, the woman was gone. But <u>hardly</u> (11) had the woman left the room when Holmes slipped across to the safe, filled his two arms with bundles of letters, and threw them all into the fire. Again, and again he did it, until the safe was empty.

Then we left the house through the garden over the garden wall. Next morning, we had breakfasted and were smoking our morning pipe, when Mr. Lestrade, of Scotland Yard, came in.

"Good morning, Mr. Holmes," he said, "I thought, perhaps you might help us in a <u>most remarkable</u> (12) case, which happened only last night at Hampstead."

"<u>Dear me</u>!" (13) said Holmes.
"What was that?"

"A murder, a most dramatic murder. Mr Milverton is the victim. Scotland Yard is looking for two criminals." „Criminals?" said Holmes. „Plural?"

Words:
(11) kaum.
(12) höchst bemerkenswert.
(13) „Ach du, meine Güte!"

"Yes, there were two of them. We have their description. The first <u>fellow</u> (14) was a bit too active, but the second was a middle-sized, strongly built man, thick neck, moustache, a black mask over his eyes."

"My, it might be a description of Watson!" said Sherlock Holmes.

"It's true," said the inspector, with amusement. "It might be a description of Watson."

"Well, I'm afraid I can't help you, Lestrade," said Holmes. "The fact is that I knew this Milverton. My sympathies are with the criminals rather than with the <u>victim</u> (15), and I will not handle in this case."

Words:
(14) Kerl.
(15) Opfer.

Working with the text

1. Before, read some background information about the author of the story

Arthur Conan Doyle was born on 22 May 1859 in Edinburgh, Scotland. He studied medicine at the University of Edinburgh. In 1880, Doyle traveled to the Arctic as a ship's doctor, and a year later to West Africa. From 1882 to 1890, he had a medical practice in Southsea, near Portsmouth. In his free time, he also wrote his first literary works. In 1887 he published the first story of detective Sherlock Holmes and his friend Dr. Watson: "A Study in Scarlet". In 1890 he moved to London.

In 1899 Doyle went to South Africa, as a doctor in the Second Boer War *(Burenkrieg)* and as a reporter for some newspapers. For these activities he was knighted as a Knight Bachelor. In 1912, Conan Doyle created his second very popular character, Professor Challenger, a researcher and explorer.

The writer was married twice and had 5 children. On 7 July 1930, Doyle died of a heart attack in Crowborough, Sussex. Sherlock Holmes writings overall: 4 novels, 56 stories and 9 Sherlock Holmes near writings (3 plays, 2 short stories, 3 essays, 1 poem). Also: Works without Holmes: 5 Professor Challenger works, 7 historical novels, 3 non-fiction books (Boer War, Congo) and 8 other works.

2. About the story:
Reading comprehension through comprehension questions

Leseverstehen – reading comprehension
Answer the questions in full sentences.

a) Where does the story take place?

b) What was Sherlock Holmes looking for in Milverton's house?

c) Who is Sherlock's "bride"? *(Braut)*

d) Who killed Milverton? And why?

e) Why did not Sherlock help Scotland Yard to find the killer?

3. Do some exercises

Quiz games about London, the location of the short story:

Exercise 1:

Do you know any famous people who are **associated** with the following London locations?

a) Buckingham Palace

b) Downing Street No 10

c) Baker Street 221B

d) Trafalgar Square (the largest square in L.)

e) Globe Theatre

f) Soho (a district in the heart of the city)

Exercise 2:

Who is who?

Eine **in London geborene** sehr berühmte Person erraten, anhand des ersten Buchstabens des Vornamens und des Nachnamens.

a) E. W.: …………………………… (born 1875)

b) C. C.: …………………………… (born 1889)

c) (Q.) E. II.: ………………………….. (born 1926)

d) R. M.: …………………………... (born 1927)

e) R. S.: ………………………….... (born 1945)

f) D. B.: …………………………… (born 1975)

Exercise 3:

Berühmte Deutsche,

die in London einige Jahre lebten.

Errate die Namen, anhand des ersten Buchstabens

des Vor- und Nachnamens:

a) G. F. H.: ……………………….. (1752 - 1759)

b) K. M.: ……………………….. (1818 - 1883)

c) P. U.: ………………………... (1921 - 2004)

d) B. B.: ………………………... (2012 - 2022)

e) H. G.: ……………………… (1998 - 2007)

Some jokes from Scotland, the author's homeland.
Schottenwitze: Schotten & Geiz

1. A Scot at the doctor. The doc: "Your wife needs sea air." The Scot took his wife and went with her to a fish shop.

2. A Scot asks his friend: "Why does Donald stand at the traffic light for hours?" He answers: "The doctor has prescribed a red light for him!"

3. A Scot visits his friend who is taking off his wallpaper from the wall. He asks: "Are you wallpapering again?" The answer: "No, we're moving into a new apartment!"

4. The traditional Scottish marriage date is February 29th. Why? The married couple only need to celebrate their wedding anniversary every 4 years.

5. Two Scots talk. William: "Is your wife economical, too?" Richard, "And how! When she has changed the water in the aquarium, there is fish soup the next day."

Short Story 2:

"The Nightingale and the Rose"

by Oscar Wilde

"She said that she would dance with me if I brought her red roses," cried the young student, "but in all my garden there is no red rose." From her nest, the Nightingale heard him, and she looked out through the leaves, and wondered.

"The Prince gives a ball tomorrow night," said the young student, "and my love will be there. If I bring her a red rose, she will dance with me <u>till dawn</u>. (1) I shall hold her in my arms, and she will lean her head upon my shoulder, and her hand will lay in mine. But there is no red rose in my garden, so I shall sit lonely, and my heart will break."

"Here, <u>indeed,</u> (2) is the true lover," said the Nightingale. And the Nightingale understood the secret of the student's sorrow, and she sat silent in the tree, and thought about the mystery of love. In the centre of the grassplot was standing a beautiful rosebush, and when she saw it, she flew over to it and landed on a branch.

"Give me a red rose," she cried, "and I will sing you my sweetest song." But the rosebush shook its head.

Words:
(1) bis zum Morgengrauen.
(2) in der Tat.

"My roses are white," it answered, "but go to my brother who grows round the old <u>sundial</u> (3), and perhaps he will give you what you want."

So, the Nightingale flew over to this rosebush. "Give me a red rose," she cried, "and I will sing you my sweetest song." But the rosebush shook its head. "My roses are yellow," it answered, "but go to my brother who grows under the student's window, and perhaps he will give you what you want." So, the Nightingale flew over to the rosebush.

"Give me a red rose," she cried, "and I will sing you my sweetest song." But the rosebush shook its head. "My roses are red," it answered, "but because of the winter and the frost and the storm I shall have no roses at all this year."

"One red rose is all I want," cried the Nightingale, "only one red rose! Is there no way by which I can get it?"

"There is a way," answered the bush, "but it is so terrible that I cannot tell it to you."
  "Tell it to me," said the Nightingale, "I am not afraid."

Words: (3) Sonnenuhr.

"If you want a red rose," said the Tree, "you must build it out of music by moonlight, and colour it with your own heart's-blood. You must sing to me with your breast against a <u>thorn</u>. (4) All night long you must sing to me, and the thorn must go through your heart, and your blood must flow into my vein and become mine."

"Love is more than life, and what is the heart of a bird compared to the heart of a man?", said the Nightingale. So, she spread her brown wings for flight and flew away. The young Student was still lying on the grass, where she had left him, and the tears were not yet dry in his beautiful eyes.

"Be happy," cried the Nightingale, "be happy, you shall have your red rose. All that I ask of you <u>in return</u> (5) is that you will be a true lover, because love is wiser than philosophy …"

The student looked up from the grass, and listened, but he could not understand what the Nightingale was saying to him. And he went into his room, and lay down on his little bed, and began to think of his love; and, after a time, he fell asleep.

Words:
(4) Dorn.
(5) im Gegenzug.

And when the moon shone in the heavens the Nightingale flew to the rosebush and set her breast against the thorn. All night long she sang with her breast against the thorn.

All night long she sang, and the thorn went deeper and deeper into her breast, and her lifeblood went away from her. And on the top of the rosebush there was blooming a <u>marvellous</u> (6) rose. But the bush cried to the Nightingale to press closer, closer against the thorn. So, the Nightingale pressed closer against the thorn, and the thorn touched her heart, and a strong pain shot through her body.

And the marvellous rose became blood-red, like the rose of the eastern sky. But the Nightingale's voice became weak, and her little wings began to beat, and a film came over her eyes. Weaker and weaker became her song.

"Look, look!" cried the rosebush, "the rose is finished now," but the Nightingale made no answer, for she was lying dead in the long grass, with the thorn in her heart. And at noon the student opened his window and looked out.

Words:
(6) wunderschön.

28

"Oh, what a wonderful piece of luck!" he cried, "here is a red rose! I have never seen any rose like it in all my life. It is so beautiful that."

Then he put on his hat and ran up to the professor's house with the rose in his hand. The daughter of the professor was sitting in the doorway, and her little dog was lying at her feet.

"You said that you would dance with me if I brought you a red rose," cried the student. "Here is the reddest rose in all the world. You will wear it tonight next your heart, and as we dance together it will tell you how I love you."

But the girl <u>frowned</u>. (7) "I am afraid it will not go with my dress," she answered, "and, besides, another young man has sent me some real jewels, and everybody knows that jewels cost much more than flowers."

"Well, you are very <u>ungrateful</u>" (8) said the student angrily. And he threw the rose into the street, where car went over it.

Words:
(7) runzelte die Stirn.
(8) undankbar.

"Ungrateful!" said the girl. "I tell you what, you are very <u>rude</u>, (9) and, after all, who are you? Only a student."

"What a silly thing love is," said the student as he walked away. "In fact, it is quite unpractical, and, as in this age to be practical is everything, I shall go back to philosophy and study metaphysics."

So, he returned to his room and pulled out a great <u>dusty</u> (10) book and began to read.

Words:
(9) grob, primitiv, unhöflich.
(10) verstaubt.

Working with the text

1. Before, read some background information about the author of the story

Oscar Wilde was born on 16 October 1854 in Dublin, Ireland, and died on 30 November 1900 in Paris. He was an Anglo-Irish writer in Victorian Great Britain. Wilde was the second of three children of a respected doctor and a translator. Through his mother's literary work, Wilde came into contact with writing at an early age.

He was a student at a boarding school. Afterwards, Wilde studied classical literature in Dublin and from 1874 in Oxford where he completed his studies with success. In 1878, his poem "Ravenna" got first public attention. Wilde moved to London, where he quickly made a name for himself as an extravagant dandy. His first works were published, and he was invited to the USA in 1881.

As a famous and celebrated poet, he married a children's book author, with whom he lived in London. They had two sons. In 1886 he lived out his homosexuality for the first time and was critical of marriage from then on.

In 1888, the fairy tale "The Nightingale and the Rose" was published in the prose collection "The Happy Prince and Other Fairy Tales".

In 1890, His best-known work, the novel "The Picture of Dorian Gray", published in 1890, was "disreputable" *(anrüchig)* for many people.

Because of his contacts with male prostitutes, Wilde was convicted *(verurteilt)* to two years in prison with hard labor *(Zwangsarbeit)* in 1895. His health was so ruined that he moved to Paris immediately after his prison time.

Wilde spent the last three years of his life impoverished and isolated in a hotel under the name "Sebastian Melmoth". Oscar Wilde died in Paris at the age of 46.

Some other literary works:
"Lord Arthur Savile's Crime"
"The Canterville Ghost"
"The Sphinx without a Secret"
 "The Selfish Giant"

2. About the story:
Reading comprehension through
comprehension questions

Your task: Read the story again and find short answers to the following questions about text content.

1. Who is the young student in love with?

2. Why is he so desperate? *(verzweifelt)*

3. A nightingale heard his sad words and wanted to help him. But how?

4. She did not have success with the first two rose bushes. Why?

5. The 3rd rose bush also saw a problem, but it had an idea to get a red rose. What problem and what idea?

6. How did the nightingale react?

7. And how did the student react?

8. What was the girl's reaction?

9. The Final:

3. Do an exercise:
A learning game.

Hier sind 8 Passagen aus der Story. In jeder Passage steckt ein Fehler.

Du hast den Text schon zweimal gelesen. Jetzt gehe den Text in Gedanken nochmals durch und finde die Fehler.

Alternativ, nochmals den gesamten Text lesen und suchen.

1. "The Prince gives a ball today night," said the young student, "and my love will be there".

2. "… If I bring her a red rose, she will kiss me. …"

3. The Nightingale flew over to this rosebush. "Give me a red rose," she cried, "and I will sing you my love song."

4. "If you want a red rose," said the Tree, "... You must sing to me with your head against a thorn".

5. "Look, look!" cried the rosebush, "the rose is finished now," but the Nightingale made no answer, for she lay sleeping in the long grass, ...

6. Then he (the student) ... ran up to the professor's house with the rose in his hand. The daughter of the professor was sitting in the doorway, and her little cat was lying at her feet.

7. "Here is the best rose in all the world. You will wear it tonight next your heart, and as we dance together it will tell you how I love you."

8. "I am afraid it will not go with my dress," she answered, "and, besides, a young prince has sent me some real jewels, and everybody knows that jewels cost much more than flowers."

Short story 3:

"A Haunted House"

by Virginia Woolf

Whatever hour you woke there was a door shutting. From room to room they went, hand in hand, lifting here, opening there, making sure - a ghostly couple. "Here we left it," she said.

And he added, "Oh, but here too!" "It's upstairs," she murmured *(to say softly)*. "And in the garden," he whispered. "Quietly," they said, "or we shall wake them." But it wasn't that you woke us. Oh, no. "They're looking for it; they're drawing *(to open)* the curtain," one might say, and so read on a page or two. "Now they've found it," one would be certain, stopping the pencil on the margin *(the edge of a line of text)*.

And then, tired of reading, one might rise and see for oneself, the house all empty, the doors standing open, only the wood <u>pigeons</u> (1) bubbling with <u>content</u> (2) and the hum of the threshing machine sounding from the farm. "What did I come in here for? What did I want to find?" My hands were empty. "Perhaps it's upstairs then?" The apples were in the <u>loft</u> (3). And so down again, the garden still as ever, only the book had slipped into the grass.

Words:
(1) Ringeltauben.
(2) Zufriedenheit.
(3) Speicher.

But they had found it in the underline drawing room (4).
Not that one could ever see them.

The windowpanes (5) reflected apples, reflected roses; all the leaves were green in the glass.

If they moved in the drawing room, the apple only turned its yellow side.

Yet, the moment after, if the door was opened, (there was something): spread (6) about the floor, hung upon the walls, pendant (7) from the ceiling — what?

My hands were empty.

The shadow of a thrush (8) crossed the carpet; from the deepest wells (9) of silence the wood pigeon drew its bubble of sound.

Words:
(4) Salon.
(5) Fensterscheiben.
(6) verteilt.
(7) herabhängend.
(8) Drossel.
(9) Quellen.

"Safe, safe, safe" the pulse of the house beat softly. "The treasure <u>buried</u> (10); the room..." the pulse stopped short. Oh, was that the buried treasure?

A moment later the light had <u>faded</u> (11). Out in the garden then? But the trees <u>spun</u> (12) darkness for a wandering <u>beam</u> (13) of sun.

The beam, I was looking for, was always burned behind the glass, so fine, so rare, coolly sunk beneath the <u>surface</u> (14).

Death was the glass; death was between us, coming to the woman first, hundreds of years ago, leaving the house, <u>sealing</u> (15) all the windows; the rooms were darkened. He left it, left her, went North, went East, saw the stars turned in the Southern sky; <u>sought</u> (16) the house, found it dropped beneath the <u>Downs</u> (17).

Words:
(10) begraben.
(11) verblasst.
(12) warfen.
(13) Strahl.
(14) unter der Oberfläche.
(15) versiegelte.
(16) suchte.
(17) Hügellandschaft.

"Safe, safe, safe," the pulse of the house beat gladly. "The Treasure yours." The wind roars up the avenue. Trees <u>stoop and bend this way and that</u>. (18) Moonbeams <u>splash and spill</u> (19) wildly in the rain.

But the beam of the lamp falls straight from the window. The candle burns <u>stiff and still</u> (20). Wandering through the house, opening the windows, whispering not to wake us, the ghostly couple seek their joy. "Here we slept," she says. And he adds, "Kisses without number."

"Waking in the morning …", "Silver between the trees …", "Up-stairs …", "In the garden …", "When summer came …", "In winter snow time …".

The doors go shutting far in the distance, gently knocking like the pulse of a heart. Nearer they come, <u>cease</u> (21) at the doorway.

Words:
(18) beugen und biegen sich hierhin und dorthin.
(19) planschen und schwappen.
(20) steif/lahm und immer noch.
(21) enden.

The wind falls, the rain slides silver down the glass. Our eyes darken, we hear no steps beside us, we see no lady spread her ghostly <u>cloak</u> (22).

His hands <u>shield</u> (23) the lantern.

"Look," he <u>breathes</u> (24).

"<u>Sound asleep</u> (25).

Love upon their lips."

<u>Stooping</u> (26), holding their silver lamp above us, long they look and deeply. Long they pause.

The wind drives straightly, the flame <u>stoops slightly</u> (27).

Words:
(22) Umhang.
(23) schützen/abschirmen
(24) haucht/atmet.
(25) tief und fest eingeschlafen.
(26) Vorgebeugt.
(27) flackert leicht.

Wild beams of moonlight cross <u>both</u> floor <u>and</u> (28) wall, and, <u>meeting, stain</u> (29) the faces; <u>the faces pondering</u> (30); the faces that <u>search</u> (31) the sleepers and <u>seek</u> (32) their <u>hidden joy</u>. (33)

"Safe, safe, safe," the heart of the house beats proudly. "Long years ..." he sighs. "Again, you found me."

"Here," she murmurs, "sleeping; in the garden reading; laughing, rolling apples in the loft. Here we left our treasure ...".

Stooping, their light lifts the lids upon my eyes. "Safe! safe! safe!" the pulse of the house beats wildly.

Waking, I cry, "Oh, is this your buried treasure? The light in the heart."

Words:
(28) sowohl als auch.
(29) treffen, färben/beflecken.
(30) die nachdenklichen Gesichter.
(31) untersuchen.
(32) begehren.
(33) verborgene Freude.

Working with the text

1. Before, read some background information about the author of the story

Virginia Woolf, an English writer, was born in Sout Kensington, London, as Virginia Stephen on 25 January 1882. She was the daughter of the writer, historian, essayist, biographer Leslie Stephen (1832–1904) and his second wife Julia Stephen (1846–1895). Virginia had three siblings *(Geschwister)* and four half-siblings from her mother's first marriage and her father's first marriage. The family home was in the London district of Kensington, 22 Hyde Park Gate. Biographers describe that her half-siblings Gerald and George sexually abused the young Virginia. The result: start of depressive illnesses.

Virginia did not go to school, but she got private lessons from tutors and her father. She was impressed by her father's literary work and his private library. As a result, she wanted to become a writer at an early age.

When her mother died on 5 May 1895, thirteen-year-old Virginia had her first mental breakdown.
On 26 June 1902, Virginia's father was made to Knight Commander of the Bath.

During this time, Virginia wrote various essays and prepared them for publication.

In January 1904, Virginia's first article was printed for The Guardian, a British daily newspaper. On 22 February 1904, her father died of cancer. In the same year, she co-founded the "Bloomsbury Group." The group brought together many artists, scientists and writers. Ten weeks after her father's death, Virginia got her second episode of mental illness, from which she could only recover at the end of the year.

In November 1904, Virginia Stephen met Leonard Woolf, who was studying law. From the end of the year until 1907, she taught English literature and history at Morley College, an educational institution for working adults. In the years up to 1909, she made several trips, including to Italy, France and Germany (Bayreuth Festival).

In August 1912, Virginia and Leonard Woolf married in London. Virginia's health condition was still weak. Her depression became stronger, and on 9 September 1913, Virginia made her first suicide attempt with sleeping pills. Nevertheless, she described her marriage as happy.

In 1915, Virginia Woolf published her first novel, "The Voyage Out," with her half-brother Gerald's publishing house. In 1917, the Woolf's founded the Hogarth Press. They specialized in modern literature from Great Britain, the USA and Russia.

Virginia's role at the Hogarth Press was to find new authors and to check their manuscripts. In July 1919, the Woolf's bought a simple cottage in Rodmell (Sussex).

In the same year, Virginia Woolfs stories "Kew Gardens" were published by their own publishing house and her second novel, "Night and Day."
In December 1922, she met the female writer Vita Sackville-West. Their friendship developed into a close love affair that lasted three years (1925–1928). In 1924, the Woolf's moved back to London-Bloomsbury.

After the United Kingdom declared war on Germany on 3 September 1939, the Woolf's decided to live in Rodmell (Sussex) again and only travel to the publishing house in London twice a month. In September 1940, the house, their London apartment and the publishing house were badly damaged by bombs during an air attack by the German Luftwaffe. Leonard Woolf was Jewish and a socialist, both feared for their lives. And Virginia was afraid of new depressions. She feared that the psychotic episodes of the past would repeat themselves, in which she heard voices and was unable to work or read.
On 28 March 1941, Virginia made suicide in the River Ouse near Rodmell.

Leonard Woolf buried her ashes under the two large elms *(Ulmen)* in the garden.

Today, busts *(Büsten)* and memorial plaques *(Gedenktafeln)* of Virginia Woolf and Leonard Woolf (he died in 1969) remember the great writer and publisher couple. Virginia Woolf was one of the most important and productive writers of modern times. She wrote 9 novels, 1 play, over 5 volumes of essays, portraits, memoirs and reviews, more than 14 volumes of diaries and letters and 46 short stories.

2. About the story:
Reading comprehension through one comprehension question

Your task: Read the story again and find an answer to the following question:

What is the **main idea** of the story?

3. Do some exercises

Exercise 1:

A learning game about the Word order =
Wortstellung in einem Satz

Erinnere dich: Für die Wortstellung in einem englischen Satz gibt es strenge Regeln.

Nun zur Aufgabe - a word puzzle
Du findest hier einzelne Wörter, die durcheinandergeraten sind. Ordne die Wörter zu einem sinnvollen Satz.

a) were loft the in apples the.

b) empty my were hands.

c) up avenue roars wind the the.

d) of the crossed carpet shadow thrush a the.

e) find to what I did want?

f) oh, the that treasure was buried?

Exercise 2:

Remember certain words

"A Haunted House" is a story with a little bit **Halloween atmosphere**.

Let us repeat some Halloween vocabulary.

Your task:
What comes in your mind if you read or hear following **Halloween Words**?

1. "The Day of the Dead"

2. "All Hallows' Eve"

3. Halloween 1991

4. Trick or Treat!

5. lighting bonfires

6. carving pumpkin

7. typical Halloween-persons, figures

8. typical Halloween things

9. spooky

10. scary (AE)

Exercise 3:

Have fun and enjoy some Halloween jokes with Q (Question) and A (Answer).

Q: A vampire is very hungry. He goes into a fast food restaurant. Do you know: What is his favourite fast food? And what will he order?

A: That is clear. He will not order anything. He is looking for a young man with a very high blood pressure.

Q: What is it, when two vampires like each other?

A: It is love at the first bite!

Q: Dracula was often in the USA. He also visited NY. What do you mean: Which building did Dracula visit in New York?

A: The Vampire State Building.

Q: Vampires also like going in cinemas. There they watch if people eat popcorn. And of course, they try to eat popcorn, too. What do you believe: Do they eat popcorn with their fingers?

A: No, they eat the fingers separately.

Short story 4:

"A Child's Christmas in Wales"

by Dylan Thomas

It was on the afternoon of the day of Christmas Eve, and I was in Mrs. Prothero's garden with her son Jim. It was snowing. It was always snowing at Christmas. In my memory, December is white as Lapland, although there were no reindeers. But there were cats. We waited to throw the cats with snowballs.

But the wise cats never appeared. We were so still. Suddenly we heard Mrs. Prothero's cry: "Fire!" "Fire!" And we ran down the garden, with the snowballs in our arms, towards the house; and smoke <u>was pouring</u> (1) out of the dining-room. We <u>bounded</u> (2) into the house, with snowballs in our hands, and stopped at the open door of the <u>smoke-filled</u> (3) room. Something was burning; perhaps it was Mr. Prothero, who always slept there after midday dinner with a newspaper over his face.

But he was standing in the middle of the room, saying, "A fine Christmas!" Then he <u>waved</u> (4) against the smoke with a <u>slipper</u> (5). "Call the fire brigade," cried Mrs. Prothero. "They will not be here," said Mr. Prothero, "it's Christmas."

Words:
(1) strömte.
(2) stürmten.
(3) rauchgefüllt.
(4) wedelte.
(5) Pantoffel.

We did not see fire, only clouds of smoke. Mr. Prothero was standing in the middle of them, waving his slipper. "Do something," he said. And we threw all our snowballs into the smoke and ran out of the house to the telephone box. "Let's also call the police," Jim said. "And the ambulance." (6) "And Ernie Jenkins, he likes fires." But we only called the fire brigade, and soon the fire engine (7) came and three tall men in helmets brought a hose (8) into the house and Mr. Prothero came out just in time before they turned it on. Nobody wanted to have a noisy Christmas Eve. And when the firemen turned off the hose and were standing in the wet, smoky room, Jim's Aunt, Miss Prothero, came downstairs.

Jim and I waited, very quietly, to hear what she would say to them. She said the right thing, always. She looked at the three tall firemen in their shining helmets, standing among the smoke and the snowballs, and she said, "Would you like anything to read?"

Years and years ago, when I was a boy, when there were wolves in Wales, when we sang all night and day in caves (9) and we chased, with bones of the English and the bears, when we rode about happy hills, it snowed and it snowed.

Words:
(6) Krankenwagen.   (7) Feuerwehrauto.
(8) Schlauch.   (9) Höhlen.

But here a small boy says, "It snowed last year, too. I made a snowman, and my brother knocked it down and I knocked my brother down and then we had tea." "Were there postmen then, too?"

"With sprinkling (10) eyes, with frozen noses and feet they went to the doors and knocked manfully. But all that the children could hear was a ringing of bells, which were inside them." "I only hear thunder sometimes, never bells." "There were church bells, too."

"Get back to the postmen." "They were just normal postmen, were loving walking and dogs and Christmas and the snow. They knocked on the doors with blue fingers ...." "Our door has got a black door knocker...." "And then they stood on the white doormat (11) and moved from foot to foot like small boys wanting to go out."

"And then the presents?" "There were the useful presents: zebra scarfs (12) of a substance like gum. And pictureless books in which small boys skated on Farmer Giles's Pond and drowned. (13) And books that told me everything about the wasp." (14)

Words:
(10) tränenden.   (11) Fußmatte.
(12) Schals.   (13) ertranken.   (14) Wespe.

"Go on to the useless presents."

"Bags of wet and many-colored <u>jelly babies</u> (15) and a <u>tram-conductor's cap</u>. (16) And a little axe, and a celluloid duck that made, when you pressed it, a most unducklike sound, and a painting book in which I could paint the grass, the trees, the sea and the animals. And troops of bright <u>tin soldiers</u>. (17) And a <u>whistle</u> (18) to make the dogs bark to wake up the old man next door. And a packet of cigarettes: you put one in your mouth and you stood at the corner of the street and you waited for hours for an old lady who <u>scold</u> (19) you for smoking a cigarette, and then with a <u>smirk</u> (20) you ate it. And then it was breakfast under the balloons."

"Were there uncles like in our house?"

"There are always uncles at Christmas. The same uncles."

Words:
(15) Gummibärchen.
(16) Straßenbahnschaffnermütze.
(17) Zinnsoldaten.
(18) Pfeife.
(19) aus/schimpfen.
(20) Grinsen.

And on Christmas mornings, I walked through the town with <u>sugar fags</u> (21), looking for news. Men and women went back from the chapel. Mistletoe hung everywhere.

And cats watched the fires. Some few large men sat in the salons, trying their new cigars, <u>coughing</u>, coughing. (22)

And some few small aunts, who were <u>not wanted</u> (23) in the kitchen and elsewhere, sat of their chairs and waited.

Not many people went through the streets on those mornings: an old man took his walk to the white bowling green and back, as he did it on Christmas, in case of rain or sunshine.

Sometimes two young men, with big pipes and without overcoats, went unspeaking down to the sea, to get appetite.

Words:
(21) Zuckerzigaretten.
(22) hustend.
(23) nicht erwünscht.

At home again, for dinner we had turkey and pudding (24), and after dinner the uncles sat in front of the fire, groaned (25) a little and slept.

Mothers, aunts and sisters rushed through the room with pots. Aunt Bessie stood at the sideboard and drank some wine. The dog was sick. Aunt Dosie had to take three aspirins, but Aunt Hannah stood in the middle of the snow-covered yard, singing like a thrush (26).

I blew up balloons to see how big they can get, and, then when they burst, which they all did, the uncles jumped up. In the afternoon, the uncles breathing like dolphins and the snow fell, I sat among garlands and Chinese lanterns and nibbled dates (27).

Or I went out with my bright new boots into the white world, on to the seaward hill, to visit Jim and Dan and Jack and to go through the still streets, leaving huge deep footprints on the pavements (28).

Words:
(24) kuchenartiger Nachtisch.
(25) stöhnten.
(26) Drossel.
(27) Datteln.
(28) Gehwege.

"I bet people will think they were <u>hippos</u>." (29) "What would you do if you saw a hippo coming down our street?" "I'd go like this, bang, bang!"

We walked on the white shore. "Can the fishes see it's snowing?" Ha, ha. We returned home through the poor streets where only a few children painted in the snow with their red fingers.

And then, at teatime, all uncles were jolly *(happy)*; and the ice cake stood in the center of the table like a <u>marble grave</u> (30). Aunt Hannah drank her tea with rum.

And now, the tall <u>tales</u> (31) that we told by the fire. I remember that we were singing Christmas carols. One, two, three, and we began to sing, with high voices.

Always on Christmas night there was music. An uncle played the fiddle, a cousin sang "Cherry Ripe" and another uncle sang "Drake's Drum."

It was very warm in the little house.

Words:
(29) Nilpferde.
(30) Marmorgrab.
(31) Märchen.

Aunt Hannah drank wine and sang a song about <u>bleeding</u> (32) hearts and the death, and then another in which she said her heart was like a Bird's Nest; and then everybody laughed again.

And then I went to bed.

I said some words to the deep and holy darkness, and then I slept.

Words:
(32) blutende.

Working with the text

1. Before, read some background information about the author of the story

Dylan Thomas was born on 27 October 1914 in Swansea, Wales. At the age of four, he was learning poems by Shakespeare and at the age of eight he was writing his first poems. At the age of eleven he published some poems in the school newspaper at his grammar school, which he left early in 1931 to work as a journalist for the South Wales Daily Post in Swansea.

He then to turn to the London artistic milieu and his other passion, alcohol.

From 1933 Dylan Thomas lived as a freelance writer in London and Wales.

In 1937 he began working for BBC London. In the same year he married the dancer Caitlin MacNamara, with whom he had three children.

He was an opponent of the war, and he did not want to do military service. So, he drank a lot of alcohol, went to the military inspection and was released.

(freigestellt).

In 1949 he and his family settled in the fishing village of Laugharne (Wales).

From 1950 onwards he did successful lecture tours to the USA.

On his fourth trip Dylan Thomas died on 9 November 1953 of pneumonia *(Lungenentzündung)* at the age of just 39.

He was buried in his Welsh hometown of Swansea.

About his literary work:

His poems are about childhood, love, sexuality, death and vision of existence.

Dylan Thomas became known to the public with his volume of poems "Deaths and Entrances", published in 1946.

During a highly successful reading tour through the United States, Dylan Thomas wrote the lyrical radio play "Under Milk Wood".

He also wrote autobiographical short stories such as "Portrait of the Artist as a Young Dog", a novel "Rebecca's Daughters" and screenplays "The Doctor and the Devils".

Dylan Thomas' first collection of poems, "Eighteen Poems", is close to surrealism. *(ist dem Surrealismus nahe)*

Some other works:
Lyrics:
"The World I Breathe"
"The Map of Love"
"In Country Sleep, And Other Poems"

Short stories and essays:
"Notebooks"
"Quite Early One Morning"
"A Child's Christmas in Wales"
"A Prospect of the Sea"
"Letters to Vernon Watkins"
"The Beach of Falesa"

Novel fragment:
"Adventures in the Skin Trade"

2. About the story:
Reading comprehension through comprehension questions

Dylan Thomas talks about his childhood memories.
(*Kindheitserinnerungen*)

Your task: Read the story again and find short answers to the following questions about his memories.

1. What terrible thing happened one afternoon on Christmas Eve?

2. Memories of Christmas presents: There were two different types of presents. Which one?

3. What was there to eat for dinner and in the afternoon on Christmas Day?

4. How was the evening on Christmas Day?

5. There are 14 animals in the story. What animals?

3. Do an interesting exercise

Playing a Pub Quiz about Wales

1. Who is the **head of state** of Wales?
   a) The First Minister of Wales   or
   b) The King of United Kingdom

2. Which animal is on the national flag of Wales?
    a) a white sheep   b) a black dog   c) a red dragon

3. Wales had a population of about …
   a) 1.1 million   b) 2.5 million   c) 3.2 million

4. The capital of Wales is …
   a) Kardiff   b) Kardif   c) Cardif   d) Cardiff

5. The highest mountain is Mount Snowdon.
   How high is it?
   a) 1.085 m   b) 915 m   c) 743 m

6. In which city was author Dylan Thomas born?
   a) Newport   b) Wrexham   c) Swansea

7. In addition to Dylan Thomas, there are other world-famous writers from Wales. One of them wrote the screenplay for the James Bond film "You Only Live Twice". Who was it?
a) Roald Dahl
b) Ken Follett
c) Kate Roberts

8. Which Welsh actor won an Oscar for his role as serial killer Hannibal Lecter in "Silence of the Lambs"?
a) Richard Burton
b) Sir Anthony Hopkins
c) Michael Sheen

9. Which Welsh pop singer sang these world hits? "She's a Lady", "Sex Bomb", "It's Not Unusual"
a) Tom Jones
b) Shakin' Stevens
c) James Fox

10. The most popular sport of the Welsh is ...
a) Hockey
b) Rugby
c) Cricket

4. Read and enjoy Welsh jokes

The school theater play

Young Dylan comes home from school and tells his mother he's been given a part in the school play. "Wonderful," says his mam. "What part is it?"
The boy reports, "I play the part of the Welsh husband." The mother says, "Oh no, go back and tell them you want a **speaking** part."

Miss and miss

Betty was born in Wales. Now she lives in London, for a short time. The nice people of London often say to her: "You miss Wales?" Betty answers: "No, **I** look nothing like her. **She** has got long blonde hair and wears a long sash." *(Schärpe)*.

Rugby first

Dai was watching a Six Nations Rugby game in Cardiff. In the full stadium there was only one empty seat, right next to him. "Is this seat free?" asked a man in the row behind. "I bought the ticket for my wife", said Dai. "But she died in an accident."
"A free seat as a mark of respect?"
"No," said Dai, "I offered it to all of my friends."
"So, and why did not they come?"
"At the moment, they are all at the funeral."

(Beerdigung)

An Englishman in the Welsh countryside

A Welsh farmer was in the field with his sheep when he saw a man drinking from a stream *(kl. Bach)* with one hand.

He shouted in Welsh, "Don't drink the water! It is disgusting! *(ekelhaft)* There is **sheep shit** in it!"
(Schafscheiße)

The man by the stream lifted his head and continued to drink. When the farmer realized that the man could not hear him, the farmer moved closer and shouted the same thing in Welsh again.

But still the man could not hear him.

Finally, the farmer walked to him and repeated his warning.

The Englishman replied, "Sorry, but I can't understand you. Can you speak English, old bimbo?" *(dummer Kerl)*

"Oh, I understand," said the farmer.
"I was just saying if you use both hands, you can drink **more** water."

Short story 5:

"The Orange of the Orphan Boy"

by Charles Dickens

When I was just a little boy, I had lost my parents and I ended up in an orphanage (1) near London at the age of nine. It was worse (2) than a prison. We had to work 14 hours a day, in the garden, in the kitchen, in the stable, in the field.

Not a day brought any change and there was only one day of rest (3) for us throughout the year: that was Christmas day. At Christmas each boy was given an orange. That was all. No candy, no toys.

But this orange was given only to those who had not done anything wrong during the year. This Christmas orange embodied the longing (4) of a whole year.

It was Christmastime again. But to my young boy's heart it almost meant the end of the world. While the other boys walked past the governor (5) of the orphanage and everyone received (6) their orange, I was forced (7) to stand in the corner and watch. It was my punishment (8) for having wanted to run away from the orphanage once.

Words:
(1) Waisenhaus.   (2) schlimmer.
(3) Ruhe.   (4) verkörperte die Sehnsucht.
(5) Direktor.   (6) erhielt.
(7) gezwungen.   (8) Strafe.

When the sharing out (9) of presents was over, the other boys were allowed to go and play in the courtyard (10). But I had to go to the sleeping room and stay in bed all day. I was very sad (11) and ashamed (12). I cried and did not want to live any longer.

After a while I heard footsteps in the room. A hand pulled away the blanket under which I had crawled away (13). I raised my eyes.

A small boy, called William, stood before my bed with an orange in his right hand and holding it out to me. I was completely flabbergasted (14).

I looked at William and then again at the fruit and I vaguely (15) felt that there had to (16) be something special about the orange.

Words:
(9) das Verteilen.
(10) Hof.
(11) traurig.
(12) beschämt.
(13) ge/verkrochen.
(14) fassungslos.
(15) vage.
(16) musste.

It suddenly <u>dawned</u> (17) on me that the orange had already been <u>peeled</u> (18). <u>Tears</u> (19) came to my eyes and when I reached out my hand. I knew I had to <u>grip tightly</u> (20) so that the orange could not fall down.

What had happened?

Ten boys <u>had joined together</u> (21) in the courtyard and decided that I too must have my orange for Christmas. So, everyone had peeled their own and cut off a <u>slice</u> (22).

They had made a new, beautiful and round orange out of 10 individual slices.

This orange was the best Christmas present in my life. It showed me how <u>comforting</u> (23) real companionship can be.

Words:
(17) dämmerte.
(18) geschält.
(19) Tränen.
(20) fest zugreifen.
(21) hatten sich zusammengefunden/-getan.
(22) Scheibe.
(23) tröstend.

Working with the text

1. Before, read some background information about the author of the story

Charles Dickens (pseudonym Boz; * 7 February 1812 in Landport near Portsmouth, England; † 9 June 1870 in Higham near Rochester, England). He was the second of eight children. In 1815 the family moved to London, shortly afterwards to Sheerness and then to Chatham in Kent. In 1822 the family returned to London because his father was transferred to the naval headquarters. Charles had a difficult childhood. His family lived lavishly *(verschwenderisch)* and had a lot of debt *(Schulden)*. Because of this, his father had to go to prison in London for several months. His mother also went to prison with seven children, which was usual *(üblich)* at the time. Only Charles, who was 12 years old at the time, lived outside the city to work in a factory to earn money for the family. His experiences there inspired some of his later books in which child working was a topic. Because of this he was no longer able to go to school regularly. After his father was released from prison in 1824, Charles returned to school until 1826. During this time, he worked in a variety of jobs, for example as a writer at a lawyer *(Rechtsanwalt)* and as a reporter in court *(Gericht)* or parliament.

In this time, he was able to study human types and to do literary studies at the British Museum. Later he wrote as a journalist for newspapers and magazines. By that, he discovered *(entdeckte)* his love of writing stories. His first publication was "Mr. Minns and his Father" in 1833, a short story from the series "Sketches by Boz". In 1836, Charles Dickens married Catherine Hogarth (1815-1879). The couple had ten children. His first novel, "The Posthumous Papers of the Pickwick Club" (The Pickwick Papers), was published in 1836/1837. This novel, written as serial stories in newspapers, made Dickens famous. No other writer had a greater influence on Dickens than William Shakespeare. In 1838, Dickens traveled to Stratford-upon-Avon and visited the house where Shakespeare was born, writing his autograph in the visitors' book. His next work, "Nicholas Nickleby" (1838-39), based on this experience. He expressed the strength *(Stärke)* of the feeling of the visitors in Shakespeare's birthplace.

His literary writing until 1870 was very extensive and varied. He wrote novels, novellas, short stories and also theater plays. Dickens undertook many reading tours in Great Britain, but also in the USA (1842 and 1867/1868), France (1846, where he met Alexandre Dumas, Victor Hugo, Théophile Gautier, among others), Italy (1844), Switzerland (1846).

These were public readings with great success. These tours and also the work on new books were very hard. On 8 June 1870, Dickens had his second stroke *(Schlaganfall)* at his country house Gads Hill Place in Higham, Kent, after working for a whole day on a new novel. He died in that house the next day, 9 June 1870, at the age of 58.

Charles Dickens was buried on 14 June 1870 in the Poets' Corner of Westminster Abbey in London.

About his works:
The English writer is one of the most important authors in world literature. Here are some examples of his best-known novels:
 "The Posthumous Papers of the Pickwick Club"
 "Oliver Twist",
 "The Life and Adventures of Nicholas Nickleby"
 "David Copperfield",
 "Great Expectations".

His short stories were also very successful, such as:
 "Sketches by Boz",
 "A Christmas Carol",
 "A Christmas Tree",
 "The Orange of the Orphan Boy",
 "The Chimes",
 "The Battle of Life".

2. About the story:
Reading comprehension through comprehension questions

Your task: Read the story again and find short answers to the following questions about the content of the short story.

1. Why was the orphanage worse than a prison?

2. How many days of rest were there?

3. What kind of gift did the boys get?

4. Did the little boy get an orange? If not, why not?

5. He had to stay in bed all day. How did he feel?

6. Ten other boys had joined together in the courtyard and decided something. What?

7. And what did the ten boys do then?

8. What did the little boy think of the action of the ten other boys?

3. Do an exercise

A learning game

Bilde aus dem Wort *orange* viele andere Wörter, bestehend aus 1 bis 5 Buchstaben. Jeder Buchstabe darf aber nur einmal innerhalb eines Wortes vorkommen.

o =

r =

a =

n =

g =

e =

Appendix – Anhang
Lösungen, Antworten - Solutions, Answers

Zur Short Story 1:
2. Reading comprehension through comprehension questions

a) The story takes place in Londen.

b) Holmes was looking for the letters with which Milverton wanted to blackmail the Earl of Dovercourt, Eva's groom *(Bräutigam)*.

c) Agatha, Milverton's housemaid, is Sherlock's "bride"

d) The Countess Albert killed Milverton because he sent blackmail letters to her husband, that broke him his heart and he died.

e) Sherlock Holmes knew this Milverton as the "worst man in London". For this reason his sympathies are with the criminals rather than with the victim.

3. Do some exercises
Exercise 1:

a) Buckingham Palace: The Queen, The King

b) Downing Street No 10: The Prime Minister of GB

c) Baker Street 221B: Sherlock Holmes

d) Trafalgar Square: Nelson's Column

e) Globe Theatre: William Shakespeare

f) Soho: Bert Brecht. Aus seiner Dreigroschenoper: „Do you see the moon over **Soho**?"

Exercise 2:

a) Edgar Wallace
b) Charlie Chaplin
c) Queen Elizabeth II.
d) Roger Moore
e) Rod Stewart
f) David Beckham

Exercise 3:

a) Georg Friedrich Händel: (1752 - 1759)
b) Karl Marx: (1818 - 1883)
c) Peter Ustinov: (1921 - 2004) *His father was the Press Attaché of the Germans Embassy, he himself grew up with a German passport)*
d) Boris Becker: (2012 - 2022)
e) Herbert Grönemeyer: (1998 - 2007)

Zur Short Story 2:
2. Reading comprehension through comprehension questions

1. Who is the young student in love with?
The student is in love with his professor's daughter.

2. Why is he so desperate? *(verzweifelt)*
In view of the ball tomorrow, he cried out in his garden: "She said she would dance with me if I brought her a red rose, but there is not a single red rose in my whole garden."

3. A nightingale heard his sad words and wanted to help him? But how?
The nightingale asked several rose bushes for a rose: "Give me a red rose and I will sing you my sweetest song."

4. She did not have success with the first two rose bushes. Why?
The 1st rose bush only had white roses. The 2nd rose bush only had yellow roses.

5. The 3rd rose bush also saw a problem, but it had an idea to get a red rose. What problem and what idea?
The red roses had frozen in the hard winter. But the frozen rose bush can produce a red rose like this:

The nightingale should sing its song of love all night long and press its heart against a rose thorn. The blood from the nightingale's heart then colours the heart of the rose red.

6. How did the nightingale react?
The nightingale was ready to die a martyr's death for the student's love. She did it as correctly as the rose bush had said.

7. And how did the student react?
The next morning, the student found the red rose and brought it to his lover.

8. What was the girl's reaction?
But she is against it and said that the rose does not match to her dress and also, that another young man has given her fantastic jewels, which are better than your flower. You are only a poor student.

9. The Final:
The student was very disappointed and threw the rose onto the street and he wanted to concentrate again on himself his studies.

3. Do an exercise: Hier die korrekten Passagen.

1. "The Prince gives a ball **tomorrow** night," said the young student, "and my love will be there".

2. "… If I bring her a red rose, she will **dance with me till dawn**. …"

3. The Nightingale flew over to this rosebush. "Give me a red rose," she cried, "and I will sing you my **sweetest song**."

4. "If you want a red rose," said the Tree, "… You must sing to me with your **breast** against a thorn".

5. "Look, look!" cried the rosebush, "the rose is finished now," but the Nightingale made no answer, for **she was lying dead** in the long grass, ….

6. Then he *(the student)* … ran up to the professor's house with the rose in his hand. The daughter of the professor was sitting in the doorway, and her little **dog** was lying at her feet.

7. "Here is the **reddest** rose in all the world. You will wear it tonight next your heart, and as we dance together it will tell you how I love you."

8. "I am afraid it will not go with my dress," she answered, "and, besides, **another young man** has sent me some real jewels, and everybody knows that jewels cost much more than flowers."

Zur Short Story 3:

2. Reading comprehension:
What is the main idea of the story?

In "A Haunted House," Virginia Woolf writes a ghost story in 1921 to describe themes of life and death, love and loss, and the importance of memory. The story is told from the perspective of the couple living in the house.

Whenever they wake up in the house, they hear noises: a door closing and the sound of a "ghost couple" that is wandering from room to room in the house.

The narrator says he can hear this ghostly couple how they are talking to each other. It is clear that they are looking for something that they left behind in the house: the "buried treasure" that the ghostly couple finally found: "the light in the heart."

"A Haunted House" seems to be Virginia Woolf's attempt to give the feeling something to sense that exists only on the edge of hearing or seeing.

3. Do some exercises

Exercise 1: A learning game about the word order.

Kurz zu den Regeln der Wortstellung im Satz:

Aussagesätze

1) Subjekt + Verb (Prädikat) + Objekt = SVO
2) Ort vor Zeit
3) Zeitangaben nie zwischen Verb und Objekt, unbetont am Ende oder Ausnahme: betont am Anfang des Satzes

Fragesätze

1) Ohne Fragewort: Hilfsverb bzw. do (does/did) vor Subjekt.
2) Mit Fragewort: Fragewort + SVO
3) Fragen werden durch das Hilfsverb verneint

Und hier die korrekten Sätze:

a) The apples were in the loft.

b) My hands were empty.

c) The wind roars up the avenue.

d) The shadow of a thrush crossed the carpet;

e) What did I want to find?

f) Oh, was that the buried treasure?

Exercise 2: Remember certain Halloween words

1. "The Day of the Dead" = „Der Tag der Toten"

A very old special tradition in **Irish life**. Its history goes back to thousands of years of Celtic life. Every year on 31st October, the Celtic people celebrated the Celtic festival of Samhain. The Irish thought that **dead people** will come back on this evening, looking for a body to live next year. So, the Irish dressed up as ghosts to drive the dead people away.

2. "All Hallows' Eve" = Vorabend der Allerheiligen
   In the 16th century the Celtic church also celebrated a religion festival, called All Hallows' Eve. From these new words were later formed: "Halloween".

3. Halloween 1991: in 1991, the Halloween tradition came from USA to Germany.

4. Trick or Treat! A very popular kid's action.
   to trick = Streich spielen, treat   = Leckerei,

5. lighting bonfires = Lagerfeuer anzünden
   A big fire should keep the evil away.

6. carving a pumpkin = ein Kürbis schnitzen: It based on legend of Jack Oldfield, the Jack-o- Lantern, who tricked the devil. The lantern was at first a turnip *(Rübe)* and later a pumpkin into burning coal.

7. typical Halloween-persons, figures: e.g., ghost, witch, devil, vampire, skeleton *(Skelett),* bones, Dracula, bat *(Fledermaus)*

8. typical Halloween things:
   candy, broom, blood, fancy dress, mask

9. spooky = gespenstisch, spukhaft, gruselig, e.g.:
   … parties, decoration, song, joke, doll,
   ergo: mehr emotional, ein bisschen kitschig

10. scary (AE) = Angst habend: erschreckend,
               furchterregend, schockierend,
   e.g.: a film, a drama, a car accident, a scary action,
      a prison is a scary thing
   ergo: auch gruselig, aber deutlich härter, mehr
      reale Actions

Zur Short Story 4:
2. Reading comprehension
Possible answers:

1. The narrator was with Jim in the Prothero family's garden. Suddenly we heard Mrs Prothero's cry: "Fire! Fire!" Smoke was pouring out of the dining room. We did not see any fire, only clouds of smoke. We threw all our snowballs into the smoke and ran out of the house to the telephone box and called the fire brigade.

2. A) There were **useful presents:** zebra scarfs, pictureless books and books that told me everything about the wasp.

B) There also were **useless presents**: Bags of wet and many-colored jelly babies, a tram-conductor's cap, a little axe, a celluloid duck, a painting book, and troops of bright tin soldiers, a whistle (to make the dogs bark *(bellen)* to wake up the old man next door), and a packet of cigarettes.

3. For dinner we had turkey and pudding. At teatime, the ice cake stood in the center of the table like a marble grave, and we had tea.

4. Always on Christmas night there was music. An uncle played the fiddle, a cousin sang "Cherry Ripe" and another uncle sang "Drake's Drum." I remember that we were singing Christmas carols.

5. And here are the 14 animals that appear in the story: reindeers, cats, wolves, bears, dogs, zebra(shawls), wasp, (celluloid)-duck, turkey, thrush, dolphins, hippos, fishes, bird's(nest).

3. Do an exercise
Play a Pub Quiz about Wales

1. Who is the **head of state** of Wales?
   b) The King of United Kingdom

2. Which animal is on the national flag of Wales?
   c) a red dragon

3. Wales had a population of about …
   c) 3.2 million

4. The capital of Wales is …
   d) Cardiff

5. The highest mountain in Wales is Mount Snowdon. How high is it?
   a) 1.085 m

6. In which city was author Dylan Thomas born?
   c) Swansea

7. In addition to Dylan Thomas, there are other world-famous writers from Wales. One of them wrote the screenplay for the James Bond film "You Only Live Twice". Who was it?
   a) Roald Dahl

8. Which Welsh actor won an Oscar for his role as serial killer Hannibal Lecter in "Silence of the Lambs"?
   b) Sir Anthony Hopkins

9. Which Welsh pop singer sang these world hits? "She's a Lady", "Sex Bomb", "It's Not Unusual"
   a) Tom Jones

10. The most popular sport of the Welsh is...
   b) Rugby

Zur Short Story 5:

2. Reading comprehension
Possible answers:

1. The boys had to work fourteen hours a day - in the garden, in the kitchen, in the stable, in the field. Not a day brought any change.

2. In the whole year, there was only one day of rest. That was Christmas Day.

3. Each boy got an orange if he hadn't done anything wrong during the year.

4. No, he didn't get an orange. He had to stand in the corner of the room and watch how the other boys get an orange each. That was his punishment for having wanted to run away from the orphanage once.

5. He was very sad and ashamed. He cried and did not want to live any longer.

6. The ten boys have decided that the little boy too must have an orange for Christmas.

7. Everyone had peeled an orange and cut off one slice. From the 10 slices they had made a new, beautiful and round orange. William gave the Christmas present to the little boy.

8. That orange was the best Christmas present of his life. It showed him how comforting real companionship can be.

3. Do an exercise: A learning game

o = or, on, one, oar *(Ruder, Riemen),* organ *(Organ, Orgel),*

r = ran, rag *(Putzlappen),* rage *(Wut, Zorn, toben),* rang *(Pastform von ring),* range *(Sortiment, Auswahl)*

a = a (car), an (orange), age, are, ago *(vor, vor langer Zeit),*

n = nag *(nörgeln),* near, no, nor *(auch nicht),*

g = gear *(FahrzeugGang),* go, gone, gran *(Oma),* groan *(stöhnen, Stöhnen)*

e = ear, earn *(verdienen),* ego (Ich, Ego), er *(Äh!),* era *(Ära)*

Let us finish: INFOs

Kurz zum Autor Rainald Bierstedt: Sachbuchautor aus Bad Saarow, bei Berlin. Fachlehrer für Englisch im (Un)Ruhestand. Leiter von Englischkursen und Golfprojekten. siehe: **www.englisch-schule-golf.de**

Übersicht über seine Ratgeber-Bücher, erschienen im Verlag Books on Demand, Norderstedt.

<u>Learn English with classic short stories</u>
Band 1: By British writers.
Copyright: 06/2025. Umfang: 96 Seiten
ISBN: 978-3-7693-7661-6

Band 2:
Copyright: in Vorbereitung 2026.
ISBN:

<u>Visuell Englisch lernen nach Themenbereichen</u>
Teil 1: Family. Home. Start the day
Copyright: 2023. Umfang: 92 Seiten
ISBN: 978-3-7578-1844-9

Teil 2: Meals and Drinks
Copyright: 02/2024. Umfang: 112 Seiten
ISBN: 978-3-7583-6717- 5

Teil 3: Christmas. Easter. Ascension. Pentecost.
Copyright: 09/2024. Umfang: 92 Seiten
ISBN: 978-3-7597-3665-9

Teil 4: Irregular verbs – unregelmäßige Verben
Copyright: 01/2025. Umfang: 124 Seiten
ISBN: 9783759720627

Englisch im deutschen Sprachgebrauch:
ÜBER ENGLISCH - DEUTSCHE WORTPAARE, DIE UNS IRRITIEREN
Copyright: 2022. Umfang: 172 Seiten
ISBN: 978-3-7557-8349-7

PSEUDO-ANGLIZISMEN IN UNSEREM ALLTAG
Copyright: 2021. Umfang: 92 Seiten
ISBN: 978-3-7526-6117-0

WIR GEHEN SHOPPEN
Copyright: 01/2020. Umfang: 144 Seiten
ISBN: 978-3-7528-3361-4

ANGLIZISMEN IN DER JUGENDSPRACHE
Copyright: 06/2020. Umfang: 112 Seiten
ISBN: 978-3-7519-5326-9

GOLF & ENGLISCH
Copyright: 2018. Umfang: 112 Seiten
ISBN: 978-3-7460-0650-5

Außerdem: Sachbücher über Golfsport:
Golf in der Schule, Golf und Olympia usw.
Siehe: www.englisch-schule-golf.de